Instructional Guides for **Literature**

THE ONE AND ONLY IVAN

A guide for the book by Katherine Applegate
Great Works Author: Jennifer Lynn Prior

SHELL EDUCATION

Image Credits

Berendje Photography and Steve Bower Shutterstock (cover; page 11)

Standards

© 2007 Teachers of English to Speakers of Other Languages, Inc. (TESOL)
© 2007 Board of Regents of the University of Wisconsin System. World-Class Instructional Design and Assessment (WIDA)
© Copyright 2010. National Governors Association Center for Best Practices and Council of Chief State School Officers.
All rights reserved.

Shell Education

5301 Oceanus Drive
Huntington Beach, CA 92649-1030
http://www.shelleducation.com

ISBN 978-1-4258-8969-2

© 2014 Shell Educational Publishing, Inc.

Table of Contents

How to Use This Literature Guide

Today's standards demand rigor and relevance in the reading of complex texts. The units in this series guide teachers in a rich and deep exploration of worthwhile works of literature for classroom study. The most rigorous instruction can also be interesting and engaging!

Many current strategies for effective literacy instruction have been incorporated into these instructional guides for literature. Throughout the units, text-dependent questions are used to determine comprehension of the book as well as student interpretation of the vocabulary words. The books chosen for the series are complex and are exemplars of carefully crafted works of literature. Close reading is used throughout the units to guide students toward revisiting the text and using textual evidence to respond to prompts orally and in writing. Students must analyze the story elements in multiple assignments for each section of the book. All of these strategies work together to rigorously guide students through their study of literature.

The next few pages describe how to use this guide for a purposeful and meaningful literature study. Each section of this guide is set up in the same way to make it easier for you to implement the instruction in your classroom.

Theme Thoughts

The great works of literature used throughout this series have important themes that have been relevant to people for many years. Many of the themes will be discussed during the various sections of this instructional guide. However, it would also benefit students to have independent time to think about the key themes of the book.

Before students begin reading, have them complete the *Pre-Reading Theme Thoughts* (page 13). This graphic organizer will allow students to think about the themes outside the context of the story. They'll have the opportunity to evaluate statements based on important themes and defend their opinions. Be sure to keep students' papers for comparison to the *Post-Reading Theme Thoughts* (page 59). This graphic organizer is similar to the pre-reading activity. However, this time, students will be answering the questions from the point of view of one of the characters in the book. They have to think about how the character would feel about each statement and defend their thoughts. To conclude the activity, have students compare what they thought about the themes before the book to what the characters discovered during the story.

Correlation to the Standards (cont.)

Standards Correlation Chart

The lessons in this book were written to support the Common Core College and Career Readiness Anchor Standards. The following chart indicates which lessons address the anchor standards.

Common Core College and Career Readiness Anchor Standard	Section
CCSS.ELA-Literacy.CCRA.R.1—Read closely to determine what the text says explicitly and to make logical inferences from it; cite specific textual evidence when writing or speaking to support conclusions drawn from the text.	Guided Close Reading Sections 1–5; Story Elements Sections 1–2, 4–5; Post-Reading Response to Literature
CCSS.ELA-Literacy.CCRA.R.2—Determine central ideas or themes of a text and analyze their development; summarize the key supporting details and ideas.	Making Connections Sections 2–3; Analyzing the Literature Sections 1–5; Guided Close Reading Sections 1–5; Post-reading Response to Literature
CCSS.ELA-Literacy.CCRA.R.3—Analyze how and why individuals, events, or ideas develop and interact over the course of a text.	Analyzing the Literature Sections 1–5; Guided Close Reading Sections 1–5; Story Elements Sections 1–3, 5; Post-Reading Response to Literature
CCSS.ELA-Literacy.CCRA.R.4—Interpret words and phrases as they are used in a text, including determining technical, connotative, and figurative meanings, and analyze how specific word choices shape meaning or tone.	Language Learning Section 1; Vocabulary Sections 1–5; Guided Close Reading Sections 1–5
CCSS.ELA-Literacy.CCRA.R.5—Analyze the structure of texts, including how specific sentences, paragraphs, and larger portions of the text (e.g., a section, chapter, scene, or stanza) relate to one another and the whole.	Vocabulary Sections 1–5; Guided Close Reading Sections 1–5
CCSS.ELA-Literacy.CCRA.R.10—Read and comprehend complex literary and informational texts independently and proficiently.	Entire Unit
CCSS.ELA-Literacy.CCRA.W.1—Write arguments to support claims in an analysis of substantive topics or texts using valid reasoning and relevant and sufficient evidence.	Reader Response Sections 2, 4; Story Elements Section 2
CCSS.ELA-Literacy.CCRA.W.2—Write informative/explanatory texts to examine and convey complex ideas and information clearly and accurately through the effective selection, organization, and analysis of content.	Reader Response Section 3
CCSS.ELA-Literacy.CCRA.W.3—Write narratives to develop real or imagined experiences or events using effective technique, well-chosen details and well-structured event sequences.	Reader Response Sections 1, 5; Story Elements Section 5

Correlation to the Standards (cont.)

Standards Correlation Chart (cont.)

Common Core College and Career Readiness Anchor Standard	Section
CCSS.ELA-Literacy.CCRA.W.4—Produce clear and coherent writing in which the development, organization, and style are appropriate to task, purpose, and audience.	Reader Response Sections 1–5; Story Elements Sections 2–3, 5; Culminating Activity
CCSS.ELA-Literacy.CCRA.W.8—Gather relevant information from multiple print and digital sources, assess the credibility and accuracy of each source, and integrate the information while avoiding plagiarism.	Culminating Activity
CCSS.ELA-Literacy.CCRA.L.1—Demonstrate command of the conventions of standard English grammar and usage when writing or speaking.	Language Learning Sections 1, 4–5; Making Connections Section 5; Culminating Activity; Post-Reading Response to Literature
CCSS.ELA-Literacy.CCRA.L.2—Demonstrate command of the conventions of standard English capitalization, punctuation, and spelling when writing.	Language Learning Sections 2–3
CCSS.ELA-Literacy.CCRA.L.4—Determine or clarify the meaning of unknown and multiple-meaning words and phrases by using context clues, analyzing meaningful word parts, and consulting general and specialized reference materials, as appropriate.	Vocabulary Sections 1–5
CCSS.ELA-Literacy.CCRA.L.6—Acquire and use accurately a range of general academic and domain-specific words and phrases sufficient for reading, writing, speaking, and listening at the college and career readiness level; demonstrate independence in gathering vocabulary knowledge when encountering an unknown term important to comprehension or expression.	Vocabulary Sections 1–5

TESOL and WIDA Standards

The lessons in this book promote English language development for English language learners. The following TESOL and WIDA English Language Development Standards are addressed through the activities in this book:

- **Standard 1:** English language learners communicate for social and instructional purposes within the school setting.
- **Standard 2:** English language learners communicate information, ideas, and concepts necessary for academic success in the content area of language arts.

About the Author—Katherine Applegate

Katherine Applegate has written many books. She writes for young adults as well as for children. She was born in Michigan, but she has lived in many places in the United States.

Applegate was inspired to write *The One and Only Ivan* after hearing the true story of a gorilla held for years in captivity. Her book won the 2013 Newbery Medal. This award is given to one book each year that is a great contribution to children's literature.

She often writes books with her husband. They are the co-authors of the Animorphs series. She lives in California and has two children. Her family has many different pets.

More information about Katherine Applegate and her books can be found at the following websites:

- http://theoneandonlyivan.com/author/
- http://www.harpercollins.com/authors/10991/Katherine_Applegate/index.aspx

Possible Texts for Text Comparisons

Have students compare the lives of Ivan, Stella, Ruby, and Bob to real animals by reading books similar to the following: *National Geographic Readers: Great Migrations Elephants* by Laura Marsh, *Gorillas* by Seymour Simon, and *A Dog's Life: Autobiography of a Stray* by Ann M. Martin.

Book Summary of *The One and Only Ivan*

Katherine Applegate writes a touching story of Ivan, a silverback gorilla, who lives in captivity at The Big Top Mall and Video Arcade. Ivan lives in a small glass cage near his elephant friend, Stella, and a stray dog named Bob.

When Ruby, a baby elephant, joins them at the Big Top Mall, Ivan promises Stella he will find a way for Ruby to live in a better place. Ivan uses his artistic abilities to help Ruby and all the animals at the Big Top Mall.

The book is based on the true story of a gorilla who lived in a cage at a mall for 27 years before going to live at a zoo in Atlanta.

Cross-Curricular Connection

This book can be used to explore concepts such as friendship, making promises, ethical treatment of animals, and the education and conservation benefits of zoos.

Possible Texts for Text Sets

- Gibbons, Gail. *Gorillas*. Holiday House, 2011.
- Laidlaw, Rob. *Wild Animals in Captivity*. Fitzhenry & Whiteside, 2008.
- Nichols, Michael, and Elizabeth Carney. *Face to Face with Gorillas*. National Geographic Children's Books, 2009.
- Wolff, Becky. *Elephants! Learn About Elephants and Enjoy Colorful Pictures*. Amazon Digital Services, 2012.

or

- Hosey, Geoff, Vicky Melfi, and Sheila Pankhurst. *Zoo Animals: Behaviour, Management, and Welfare*. Oxford University Press, 2013.
- Nyhuis, Allen W., and Jon Wassner. *America's Best Zoos: A Travel Guide for Fans & Families*. The Intrepid Traveler, 2008.
- Robinson, Phillip T. *Life at the Zoo: Behind the Scenes with the Animal Doctors*. Columbia University Press, 2007.

Name _____ Date _____

Pre-Reading Theme Thoughts

Directions: For each statement, draw a picture of a happy face or a sad face. Your face should show how you feel about each statement. Then, use words to show why you feel that way.

Statement	How Do You Feel? ☺ ☹	Why Do You Feel That Way?
Animals should be kept in cages.		
Animals that perform at circuses are fun to watch.		
A zoo is a good place for a wild animal to live.		
Animals are able to have friends.		

Ivan at the Big Top Mall (pages 1–60)

Vocabulary Overview

Key words and phrases from this section are provided below with definitions and sentences about how the words are used in the story. Introduce and discuss these important vocabulary words with students. If you think these words or other words in the story warrant more time devoted to them, there are suggestions in the introduction for other vocabulary activities (page 5).

Word	Definition	Sentence about Text
silverback (p. 2)	an adult gorilla	Ivan is a mighty **silverback**.
majestic (p. 4)	grand or wonderful	His shadow is **majestic**.
domain (p. 7)	territory or home	Ivan's **domain** is made of glass, metal, and cement.
jungle (p. 7)	a tropical forest with many plants and trees	His domain is painted to look like a **jungle**.
imagination (p. 20)	creative thinking	People don't think a gorilla can have **imagination**.
shackles (p. 31)	handcuffs for the legs or arms	There are **shackles** on the elephant's legs.
undaunted (p. 37)	not afraid	He is **undaunted** by anything.
philosopher (p. 51)	a great thinker	Gorillas are **philosophers**.
juvenile (p. 53)	a child; a young creature	Ivan was captured as a **juvenile**.
expression (p. 57)	emotion shown on the face	He has an angry **expression**.

Name _____ Date _____

Vocabulary Activity

Directions: Draw lines to complete the sentences.

Beginnings of Sentences	Endings of Sentences
The Big Top Mall	to draw pictures.
Ivan is a mighty	**silverback**.
He was captured when	he was a **juvenile**.
He lives in a **domain**	is nothing like a **jungle**.
Julia uses her **imagination**	at the Big Top Mall.

Directions: Answer this question.

1. What are three things that Ivan likes best about his jungle domain at the Big Top Mall?

_____

_____

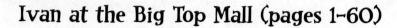
Ivan at the Big Top Mall (pages 1–60)

Analyzing the Literature

Provided below are discussion questions you can use in small groups, with the whole class, or for written assignments. Each question is written at two levels so you can choose the right question for each group of students. For each question, a few key points are provided for your reference as you discuss the book with students.

Story Element	Level 1	Level 2	Key Discussion Points
Character	Where do elephants and gorillas naturally live?	How do you think the elephant and gorilla feel about living at the Big Top Mall instead of their natural environments?	Elephants and gorillas naturally live in grasslands and jungles. Stella and Ivan are captured and taken away from their homes to perform in the circus and at the Big Top Mall. They are probably unhappy and would like to be in their natural environments.
Character	Bob is the one animal who made a choice to live at the Big Top Mall. Why does he like it there?	How is Bob's life at the Big Top Mall different from that of the other animals?	Bob is abandoned on a freeway when he is a puppy and has no place to go. Finding the Big Top Mall is good for him because he has access to food and a warm place to sleep. He is not kept in a cage like the other animals and can come and go as he pleases. At the Big Top Mall, Bob is safe and has friends.
Setting	Describe Ivan's domain.	Describe how Ivan feels about his domain.	Ivan's domain is small and is painted to look like a jungle on one wall. The other three walls are glass. It has a small pool of dirty water. Ivan gets bored in his domain. He probably wishes he had more space and more things to do.
Setting	How is Ivan's domain different from living in a jungle?	What do you think Ivan wants to change about where he lives?	A jungle has trees, clean water, fresh air, and fresh food. A jungle also has other gorillas. Ivan probably wants his domain to be more like a real jungle, but really, Ivan would probably be happiest if he were not in captivity at all.

Name _____ Date _____

Reader Response

Think

At the Big Top Mall, Ivan is not happy in his domain, but he has two very dear friends— Stella and Bob.

Narrative Writing Prompt

Write about your best friends and how they help you feel better in sad times.

_____

_____

_____

_____

_____

_____

_____

_____

_____

Name _____ Date _____

Guided Close Reading

Closely reread about Ivan and the drawings he makes (pages 15–20).

Directions: Think about these questions. In the space below, write ideas or draw pictures as you think. Be ready to share your answers.

---

❶ What text helps you understand how Ivan feels about drawing pictures?

---

❷ Explain the differences between Julia's drawings and Ivan's drawings.

---

❸ Based on the story, how does Ivan feel about his art?

Name _____ Date _____

Making Connections–Being an Artist

Directions: Julia draws pictures of ideas in her head. Ivan draws pictures of things he can see in his cage. In the first box below, draw a picture of something you can see near you right now. In the second box, draw a picture of an idea that is in your mind. Describe each picture in a sentence.

_____   _____

_____   _____

_____   _____

_____   _____

Name _____ Date _____

Language Learning–Metaphors

Directions: Rewrite each simile below to make it a metaphor. The first one has been done for you.

Language Hints!

- Ivan says that Stella is a mountain. That is a **metaphor**. She is not really a mountain. He just means she is really big.

- Ivan could have said Stella is as big as a mountain. That is a **simile** because it uses the words *like* or *as*.

1. Stella is as big as a mountain.

   Stella is a mountain. _____

2. Bob is as small as a mouse.

   _____

3. The seal acts like a clown.

   _____

4. The sun bear is as soft as a cottonball.

   _____

5. The gorilla is as playful as an otter.

   _____

Name _____ Date _____

Story Elements—Character

Directions: Ivan, Stella, and Bob are all friends at the Big Top Mall. Think about what you know about them.

	Ivan	Stella	Bob
Where does he or she come from?			
How does he or she end up at the Big Top Mall?			
What is something special about him or her?			
List one or two things he or she likes at the Big Top Mall.			
Write three words to describe him or her.			

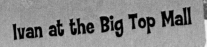

Name _____ Date _____

Story Elements-Setting

Directions: The Big Top Mall is a small circus. Animals perform and they have cages or domains where they live. Each animal has a different kind of domain. In the box below, draw a map of how you imagine the Big Top Mall looks. Include the performance area, the animal domains, and the keeper's office.

Ruby and Stella (pages 61–120)

Vocabulary Overview

Key words and phrases from this section are provided below with definitions and sentences about how the words are used in the story. Introduce and discuss these important vocabulary words with students. If you think these words or other words in the story warrant more time devoted to them, there are suggestions in the introduction for other vocabulary activities (page 5).

Word	Definition	Sentence about Text
nuzzling (p. 75)	cuddling	Stella is **nuzzling** the baby elephant.
pout (p. 75)	look sad	Ivan **pouts** when he doesn't get attention from Stella.
grumbles (p. 75)	complains	Bob **grumbles** when his sleep is disturbed.
heritage (p. 79)	background, traits that are passed down	Bob is not sure of his family **heritage**.
moaning (p. 95)	softly groaning or crying	Stella is **moaning** from the pain in her foot.
opportunity (p. 97)	a chance	Stella did not have the **opportunity** to have babies.
contemplating (p. 97)	thinking deeply	She is **contemplating** what it would be like to be a mother.
captured (p. 103)	took as a prisoner	Humans **captured** Ruby and took her to the circus.
unpredictable (p. 104)	not to be understood or anticipated	Humans can be very **unpredictable**.
addled (p. 112)	confused	Stella is **addled** by pain.

Name _____ Date _____

Vocabulary Activity

Directions: Choose at least two words from the story. Draw a picture that shows what these words mean. Label your picture.

Words from the Story

nuzzling	pout	grumbles	heritage	moaning
opportunity	contemplating	captured	unpredictable	addled

Directions: Answer this question.

1. Besides **nuzzling**, what does Stella do to show Ruby that she cares for her?

_____

Ruby and Stella (pages 61–120)

Analyzing the Literature

Provided below are discussion questions you can use in small groups, with the whole class, or for written assignments. Each question is written at two levels so you can choose the right question for each group of students. For each question, a few key points are provided for your reference as you discuss the book with students.

Story Element	Level 1	Level 2	Key Discussion Points
Character	How does Stella know a baby elephant is coming to the Big Top Mall?	Why isn't Stella happy that a baby elephant is coming to live with her?	Stella says she can hear the baby elephant crying for its mother. She is probably not happy because she knows the baby has been taken from its family. She also knows that the living conditions at the Big Top Mall are not good.
Setting	What does Ruby say she did every day when she was with the circus?	How is the Big Top Mall different from where Ruby lived with the circus?	Ruby says there were other elephants at the circus. Every day they walked in a circle and ate breakfast and then their feet were chained up. At the Big Top Mall, the animals live in small cages and they do not get out to move around unless they are performing in a show.
Plot	What promise does Ivan make to Stella?	Why does Ivan think that keeping the promise will be harder than trying not to be a gorilla anymore?	Ivan promises that he will take care of Ruby and that he will somehow give her a better life. Ivan is not sure he can do that for Ruby because he does not even know how he can save himself from his life of captivity. He is probably going to try to think of a way to help her.
Character	How does Ivan feel when Stella dies?	How does Ivan describe his feelings after Stella dies?	Ivan is very sad to lose Stella. He wishes his heart could be made of ice so he would not have to feel the sadness. He says it feels like he has forgotten how to breathe. Stella was such an important part of Ivan's life that he probably does not feel like himself now that she is gone.

Name _____ Date _____

Reader Response

Think

Ivan makes a promise to Stella that he will take care of Ruby and keep her from having a life at the Big Top Mall in a cage. Ivan is not sure how he is going to keep his promise.

Opinion Writing Prompt

What do you think Ivan can do to get Ruby to a better place? Write about what you think Ivan should do to keep her safe and give her a better life than Stella had.

_____

_____

_____

_____

_____

_____

_____

_____

_____

_____

Name _____ Date _____

Guided Close Reading

Closely reread the story Stella tells about Jambo (pages 63–66).

Directions: Think about these questions. In the space below, write ideas or draw pictures as you think. Be ready to share your answers.

1 How do you know Ivan likes stories with happy endings?

2 In what way does Stella describe a good zoo?

3 What words in Stella's story show that Jambo wanted to protect the little boy?

Name _____ Date _____

Making Connections-Freedom and Captivity

Directions: Living in captivity means being taken from home and not being able to get back. Animals that live in the wild have very different lives from animals that live in cages or in zoos. Sort these living conditions into two groups: *Living in the Wild* and *Living in Captivity*.

Living in the Wild	Living in Captivity

Not much contact with other animals

Food provided

Space to move around

Kept behind bars or glass

Human-made surroundings

Have to find food

Contact with other wild animals

Stuck in a small area

Natural surroundings

Free to do as they please

#40101—Instructional Guide: The One and Only Ivan

Name _____ Date _____

Language Learning-Capitalization

Directions: Rewrite each sentence. Use proper capitalization.

Language Hints!

- Use a capital letter at the beginning of each sentence.
- Use a capital letter for each name or other proper noun.

1. stella and ruby become friends.

   _____

2. ivan lives at the big top mall.

   _____

3. julia gives ivan paper and crayons.

   _____

4. ivan was born in africa.

   _____

5. the real ivan lived at zoo atlanta.

   _____

6. ruby loves stella like a mother.

   _____

Name _____ Date _____

Story Elements-Plot

Directions: Ruby is afraid to get out of the truck until she sees Stella. When the elephants are together, they twirl their trunks together, flap their ears, and sway back and forth. Ruby holds on to Stella's tail. Draw a picture showing Ruby and Stella together.

Name _____ Date _____

Story Elements-Character

Directions: Ivan pouts when he sees Ruby and Stella together. Pretend you are Ivan and write a letter to Stella telling her how you feel.

Dear Stella,

_____

_____

_____

_____

_____

_____

_____

_____

_____

Sincerely,

Ivan

Keeping the Promise (pages 121–179)

Vocabulary Overview

Key words and phrases from this section are provided below with definitions and sentences about how the words are used in the story. Introduce and discuss these important vocabulary words with students. If you think these words or other words in the story warrant more time devoted to them, there are suggestions in the introduction for other vocabulary activities (page 5).

Word	Definition	Sentence about Text
unsuspecting (p. 123)	unaware	Ivan's **unsuspecting** father does not know what he and Tag are doing.
tolerant (p. 123)	able to put up with	The big gorilla is **tolerant** with the babies.
scowl (p. 126)	an unpleasant expression	Ivan's father wears a **scowl** on his face.
glamorous (p. 132)	exciting and attractive	At first, Ivan lives a **glamorous** life in the human world.
dignity (p. 142)	self-respect	Ivan tries to move with **dignity**.
dozing (p. 154)	sleeping	Ruby is **dozing** after a long day of training.
encouraging (p. 159)	inspiring confidence	Ivan tries to be **encouraging** to Julia.
scornful (p. 162)	full of dislike	Bob's laugh is **scornful**.
amends (p. 166)	to make right	The humans want to make **amends** to the animals.
annoyance (p. 176)	irritation	Ruby shows **annoyance** with the ropes around her feet.

Name _____ Date _____

Vocabulary Activity

Directions: Cut apart these sentence strips. Put the sentences in order. Use the story to help you.

Ivan tries to look **encouragingly** at Julia's painting.

Ruby is **dozing** after she hits Mack with her trunk.

Ruby shows **annoyance** at the ropes on her feet.

Bob gives a **scornful** laugh about Mack getting hit.

Ivan tells Ruby that zoos are humans' way of making **amends**.

Keeping the Promise (pages 121-179)

Analyzing the Literature

Provided below are discussion questions you can use in small groups, with the whole class, or for written assignments. Each question is written at two levels so you can choose the right question for each group of students. For each question, a few key points are provided for your reference as you discuss the book with students.

Story Element	Level 1	Level 2	Key Discussion Points
Character	What does Ivan remember about being with his family?	How do you think Ivan feels when he remembers his family?	Ivan remembers how he and his sister were named. He remembers how they played and jumped on their father. He also remembers when the humans killed his mother and father. He is happy when he remembers his family, but he is sad that he is not with them anymore.
Character	What does Ruby do when Mack tries to train her?	Why do you think Ruby does not move when Mack tells her to?	Ruby refuses to move. She sits down and will not do what Mack says. When Mack swings a stick at her, she knocks him down with her trunk and hurts him. She probably does not like Mack telling her what to do, so when she gets tired she becomes stubborn.
Plot	What new thing does Julia bring to Ivan?	What does Ivan think of the fingerpaints?	Julia brings fingerpaints to Ivan. He is fascinated with the paints because the colors are bright and they spread out on the paper.
Plot	What project does Ivan begin to work on at night?	How do you think Ivan's project will help him keep his promise to Stella?	Ivan begins painting at night. He makes many paintings on several sheets of paper. He is probably going to use his artwork to help get Ruby to a better place.

Name _____ Date _____

Reader Response

Think

Ivan tries to think of a plan to help Ruby. He wants her to live in a zoo, so he begins a project with his paintings. He hopes his plan will solve the problem of Ruby living her life in a cage.

Informative/Explanatory Writing Prompt

Think of a time when you needed to solve a problem. Describe the steps you took to solve your problem. Did your plan work?

_____

_____

_____

_____

_____

_____

_____

_____

_____

Name _____ Date _____

Guided Close Reading

Closely reread about Ruby's training with Mack and what happens afterward (pages 148–156).

Directions: Think about these questions. In the space below, write ideas or draw pictures as you think. Be ready to share your answers.

❶ Use the text to describe how Bob feels about Mack and how he treats Ruby.

❷ Based on the story, how do you know that Julia and George hope that Mack will treat Ruby better?

❸ What text shows that George does not feel sorry for Mack when Ruby hits him with her trunk?

Name _____ Date _____

Making Connections-Promises, Promises

Directions: Think about a time when you made a promise to a friend or a family member. Answer the questions about your promise.

1. What was the promise?

    _____

    _____

2. To whom did you make the promise?

    _____

    _____

3. Why did you make this promise?

    _____

    _____

4. Why was the promise important to keep?

    _____

    _____

5. How did you keep your promise?

    _____

    _____

Name _____ Date _____

Language Learning-Quotation Marks

Directions: Quotation marks are used to show the words that characters say. Rewrite each sentence using quotation marks.

Language Hints!

- Put quotation marks around the words spoken by the characters.
- Commas separate the quotation from the rest of the sentence.

1. I can help Ruby, says Ivan.

_____

2. Stella says, Humans are unpredictable.

_____

3. I'm happy Ruby hit Mack, Bob growls.

_____

4. Dad, come see what Ivan created, exclaims Julia.

_____

_____

5. We've faced a lot together, Ivan, says Mack.

_____

_____

Name _____ Date _____

Story Elements-Characters

Directions: Bob and Ivan watch as Mack tries to train Ruby. Bob snarls. He laughs when Mack gets hurt. If Bob could talk to Mack, what do you think he would say? Draw a picture of the scene. Use speech bubbles to show what Bob would say to Mack.

#40101—Instructional Guide: The One and Only Ivan

39

Name _____ Date _____

Story Elements–Characters

Directions: Ivan promises Stella that he will somehow make sure Ruby does not have to live out her life at the Big Top Mall. He tries to think of a plan. Pretend you are Ivan. Describe your plan using this flow chart to show all the steps.

```
┌─────────────────────────────────────────────┐
│                                               │
│                                               │
│                                               │
│                                               │
│                                               │
└─────────────────────────────────────────────┘
                      │
                      ▼
┌─────────────────────────────────────────────┐
│                                               │
│                                               │
│                                               │
│                                               │
│                                               │
└─────────────────────────────────────────────┘
                      │
                      ▼
┌─────────────────────────────────────────────┐
│                                               │
│                                               │
│                                               │
│                                               │
│                                               │
└─────────────────────────────────────────────┘
```

The Plan Works! (pages 179–240)

Vocabulary Overview

Key words and phrases from this section are provided below with definitions and sentences about how the words are used in the story. Introduce and discuss these important vocabulary words with students. If you think these words or other words in the story warrant more time devoted to them, there are suggestions in the introduction for other vocabulary activities (page 5).

Word	Definition	Sentence about Text
gnaws (p. 181)	chews	Bob **gnaws** at his tail.
spacious (p. 189)	with lots of room	Bob thinks Ivan's belly is **spacious**.
temperamental (p. 191)	sensitive; likely to change moods quickly	Bob thinks Ivan is a **temperamental** artist.
monstrosity (p. 197)	something that is huge and not nice to look at	The billboard is a **monstrosity**.
sullenly (p. 200)	unhappily	Ruby walks **sullenly** during the show.
disarray (p. 211)	not in order	Ivan's paintings are on the floor in **disarray**.
coincidence (p. 215)	something that happens by chance or by accident	George thinks Ivan's word might be a **coincidence**.
publicity (p. 218)	attention with the public	A billboard brings **publicity**.
principle (p. 220)	doing the right thing	It is a matter of **principle**.
protestors (p. 235)	people who are not in favor of something	The **protestors** carry signs in the parking lot.

Name _____ Date _____

Vocabulary Activity

Directions: Complete each sentence below. Use one of the words listed.

Words from the Story

protestors	publicity	coincidence	spacious
gnaws	monstrosity	principle	disarray

1. The billboard sign is a _____.

2. The billboard brings _____ to Ruby.

3. Saving Ruby is a matter of _____.

4. The _____ are angry that Ruby lives in a cage.

Directions: Answer this question.

5. How do you think Ivan will feel when Ruby is taken to a **spacious** zoo?

_____

_____

_____

_____

The Plan Works! (pages 179–240)

Analyzing the Literature

Provided below are discussion questions you can use in small groups, with the whole class, or for written assignments. Each question is written at two levels so you can choose the right question for each group of students. For each question, a few key points are provided for your reference as you discuss the book with students.

Story Element	Level 1	Level 2	Key Discussion Points
Setting	Ivan sees an advertisement on TV about the zoo. What is the elephant's home like at the zoo?	How is the zoo environment similar to and different from an elephant's home in the wild?	Ivan sees that the elephants live in a place with trees and they are outside. There are many elephants living together. It is similar to their home in the wild because they have room to move and there is fresh air and trees. It is different because there are walls and they are not truly free.
Character	To whom does Ivan want to give his paintings?	Why does Ivan think Julia should be the first person to see his work?	Ivan gives his paintings to Julia. He thinks she will understand because she is an artist. He thinks she might take the time to put the painting together and figure out his message. He is right!
Character	Who helps Ivan show the painting message to Julia?	Why do you think Bob wants to help Ivan?	Bob helps Ivan by holding up some of the paintings in his mouth. Bob does not like the humans. He is not happy that Ivan, Stella, Ruby, and the others were captured. Ivan is Bob's friend, and Bob wants to help Ivan fulfill his promise.
Plot	What happens as a result of the new billboard and the article in the newspaper?	Why do you think Julia wants to put Ivan's painting on the billboard?	Lots of people take interest in the animals at the Big Top Mall. Julia is probably hoping that attention to the place will result in Ruby going to a zoo and not being mistreated by Mack anymore.

Name _____ Date _____

Reader Response

Think

Ivan does not want Ruby to live at the Big Top Mall. He wants her to be in a place where she has space to move around and where she can live with other elephants.

Opinion Writing Prompt

What do you think about animals living in captivity? Write your opinion about whether or not animals should be captured in the wild to live at a circus or in a zoo.

_____

_____

_____

_____

_____

_____

_____

_____

_____

Name _____ Date _____

Guided Close Reading

Closely reread about Ivan getting Julia's attention for his puzzle of paintings (pages 207–220).

Directions: Think about these questions. In the space below, write ideas or draw pictures as you think. Be ready to share your answers.

---

❶ Gorillas beat their chests when they are trying to protect something. Use the text to describe what else Ivan does to get the attention of Julia and her father.

---

❷ What does Julia see in Ivan's painting that proves his picture is of Ruby at the zoo?

---

❸ How do you know that George is afraid Mack will not be happy about the new billboard?

Name _____ Date _____

Making Connections-Getting Publicity

Directions: Billboards are used to draw attention to different things. Some billboards tell about stores. Some billboards tell about restaurants. Others draw attention to events. Think of something you would like to advertise on a billboard. It could be a school event or a favorite location. You could even announce the arrival of a new brother or sister. Draw your billboard below.

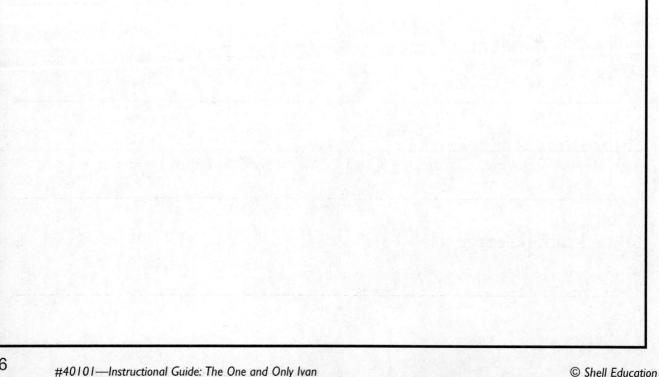

Name _____ Date _____

Language Learning-Possessives

Directions: Rewrite each phrase below using a possessive. The first one has been done for you.

Language Hints!

- A possessive is a word that shows ownership.

- For example, Ruby is *Ivan's* friend. Ruby is the friend who belongs to Ivan.

1. the friend of Ivan

   Ivan's friend _____

2. the crayons that belong to Julia

   _____

3. the cage that belongs to Stella

   _____

4. the Big Top Mall that belongs to Mack

   _____

5. the trunk that belongs to Ruby

   _____

6. the broom George uses

   _____

Name _____ Date _____

Story Elements—Setting

Directions: Julia describes what she sees in Ivan's painting on pages 212–216. Draw the billboard painting that Julia describes with the picture and the word Ivan spelled.

Name _____ Date _____

Story Elements-Plot

Directions: Complete the story map with the events that happened, starting with George putting up the billboard and ending with the woman from the zoo visiting Ruby.

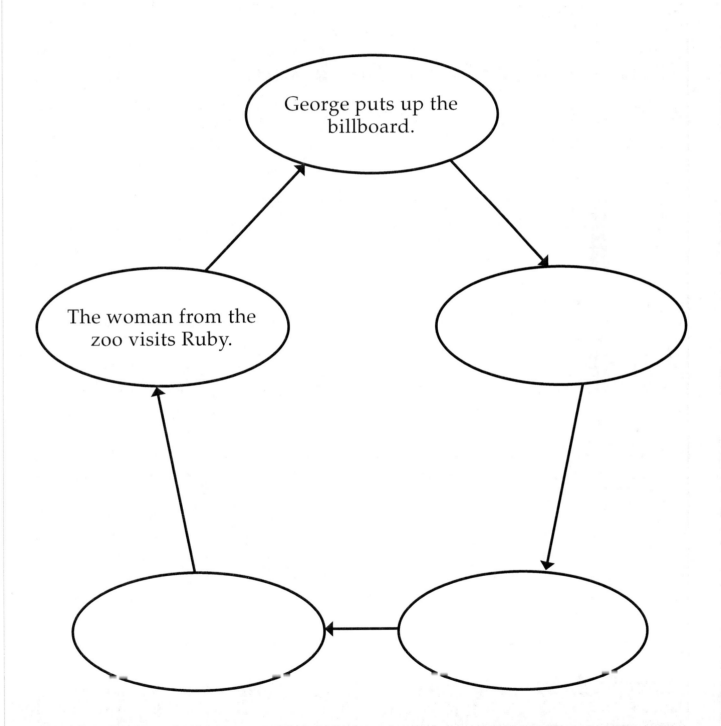

George puts up the billboard.

The woman from the zoo visits Ruby.

A New Life for All (pages 241–300)

Vocabulary Overview

Key words and phrases from this section are provided below with definitions and sentences about how the words are used in the story. Introduce and discuss these important vocabulary words with students. If you think these words or other words in the story warrant more time devoted to them, there are suggestions in the introduction for other vocabulary activities (page 5).

word	Definition	Sentence about Text
retreats (p. 241)	pulls back; leaves	The doctor **retreats** when Ivan beats his chest.
survivor (p. 246)	one who succeeds despite hardship	George says Bob is a **survivor**.
determined (p. 256)	having a purpose	The people in white coats look **determined**.
contented (p. 268)	happy; satisfied	The gorillas on the TV are **contented**.
placid (p. 268)	peaceful; calm	The gorilla family is **placid**.
socialize (p. 275)	interact with others	Ivan is afraid to **socialize** with the other gorillas.
cower (p. 278)	crouch in fear	Ivan **cowers** when he is afraid.
relent (p. 282)	give in	Ivan **relents** when Maya calls him back to the glass cage.
habitats (p. 289)	environments; places to live	There are many **habitats** for different animals at the zoo.
beckoning (p. 296)	calling	One of the keepers is **beckoning** to Ivan.

Name _____ Date _____

Vocabulary Activity

Directions: Practice your writing skills. Write at least three sentences using words from the story.

Words from the Story

retreats	survivor	determined	contented	placid
socialize	cower	relent	habitats	beckoning

_____

_____

_____

_____

_____

_____

_____

Directions: Answer this question.

1. Why do you think Ivan **cowers** and does not **socialize** with the other gorillas at first?

_____

_____

A New Life for All (pages 241-300)

Analyzing the Literature

Provided below are discussion questions you can use in small groups, with the whole class, or for written assignments. Each question is written at two levels so you can choose the right question for each group of students. For each question, a few key points are provided for your reference as you discuss the book with students.

Story Element	Level 1	Level 2	Key Discussion Points
Characters	What do the people from the zoo do to get Ruby and Ivan comfortable with the boxes?	Why don't the zoo people just push Ruby and Ivan into the boxes?	The people from the zoo try to coax Ruby and Ivan into the boxes using a clicker and treats. They probably do not want to frighten them. They want to treat them humanely and not cause them to be fearful as they are moved to their new homes.
Characters	What does Ruby say to Ivan when she gets into the box?	Why is Ruby afraid to leave the Big Top Mall to live at the zoo?	Ruby says she is afraid and that she doesn't want to leave Ivan. The Big Top Mall is not a good place to live but Ruby is familiar with it and she has friends. She doesn't know if the other elephants at the zoo will like her.
Plot	Where is Ivan first taken at the zoo?	Why do you think Ivan is put in a cage at first and not put in with the other gorillas right away?	Ivan is taken to a clean cage at the zoo. They probably want to help him adjust to living with other gorillas, so they have him watch the gorillas on a TV. Then, they let him see the other gorillas through the glass. The gorillas need time to get used to each other.
Setting	How is Ivan's new home different from the Big Top Mall?	How is Ivan's new home similar to the home he was taken from as a baby?	Ivan's new home at the zoo gives him more freedom and space to move around. It has an outdoor area with trees, grass, and bugs. There are other gorillas there. It still has walls and is a cage of sorts, but it is more like his natural home.

Name _____ Date _____

Reader Response

Think

In Ivan's new home at the zoo, he has a new family of gorillas. They play tag. They lie in the sun. They pick bugs off each other.

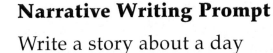

Narrative Writing Prompt

Write a story about a day in Ivan's life with his new family.

_____

_____

_____

_____

_____

_____

_____

_____

_____

_____

_____

Name _____ Date _____

Guided Close Reading

Closely reread about Ivan's move from the cage into the gorilla habitat (pages 280–284).

Directions: Think about these questions. In the space below, write ideas or draw pictures as you think. Be ready to share your answers.

---

1 In what ways does Ivan show the juvenile and the other gorillas that he is a silverback?

---

2 What part of the story shows that Ruby is enjoying her new home at the zoo?

---

3 How does the reader know that Kinyani is inviting Ivan to play tag?

Name _____ Date _____

Making Connections-The Great Outdoors

Directions: Ivan sees all kinds of new things in his new habitat at the zoo. Write the words below in alphabetical order.

Word Bank

sky	grass	tree	ant	bird
dirt	cloud	wind	flower	rock

1. _____

2. _____

3. _____

4. _____

5. _____

6. _____

7. _____

8. _____

9. _____

10. _____

Name _____ Date _____

Language Learning-Superlative Adjectives

Directions: Rewrite each sentence adding *-est* to the end of the adjective.

Language Hints!

- Superlatives are used to compare one person or thing to two or more other people or things.

- When *–est* is added to the end of an adjective it makes a superlative adjective.

1. This elephant is big.

   This elephant is biggest.
   _____

2. That giraffe is tall.

   _____

3. Bob is the small dog.

   _____

4. This gorilla is old.

   _____

5. Ruby is young.

   _____

6. Mack is mean.

   _____

7. Stella's tail is long.

   _____

Name _____ Date _____

Story Elements–Characters

Directions: Ruby and Ivan are no longer together, but Ivan is happy that Ruby has a nice, safe home. Pretend you are Ruby and write a letter to Ivan telling him about your new home at the zoo.

Dear Ivan,

_____

_____

_____

_____

_____

_____

_____

_____

_____

_____

Sincerely,
Ruby

Name _____ Date _____

Story Elements-Plot

Directions: Bob says he wants to stay wild and not have a home. In the end, Bob ends up living with Julia and her family. On the lines below, write a new part of the story telling about how Bob ended up living with Julia.

_____

_____

_____

_____

_____

_____

_____

_____

_____

_____

_____

_____

Post-Reading Theme Thoughts

Directions: Choose a main character from *The One and Only Ivan*.
Pretend you are that character. Draw a picture of a happy face or a
sad face to show how the character would feel about each statement.
Then, use words to explain your picture.

Character I Chose _____

Statement	How Does the Character Feel? ☺ ☹	What Does the Character Think?
Animals should be kept in cages.		
Animals that perform at circuses are fun to watch.		
A zoo is a good place for a wild animal to live.		
Animals are able to have friends.		

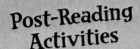
Culminating Activity: Remembering Ivan

Directions: Read about the real gorilla named Ivan. Then, complete the activity below.

The Real Ivan

Ivan was a real gorilla. He and his sister were taken from the wild as babies. His sister died soon after. Ivan lived with a family for five years. He was then given to a mall where he was kept in a small cage for 27 years. After a story about him was published in *National Geographic* magazine, the public came to Ivan's rescue. He went to live at Zoo Atlanta in 1994. Ivan interacted with his new family of gorillas, but he was always more bonded to his keepers than to the other gorillas. Ivan died in 2012 at the age of 50.

Animals are often taken from the wild and used for human entertainment. Make a list below of different ways animals are used. Then, make a list of things humans could do for entertainment instead.

Animal Entertainment	**Other Kinds of Entertainment**
_____	_____
_____	_____
_____	_____
_____	_____
_____	_____

Culminating Activity: Remembering Ivan (cont.)

Directions: Read about the purpose of zoos. Then, complete the Venn diagram about zoos below.

The Purpose of Zoos

Even though zoo animals live in captivity, a good zoo serves an important purpose. Many animal species that have been close to extinction have been saved through breeding programs. Zoos also serve to educate the public about animals and the environment. The more people know about wild animals and what they need to survive in nature, the better off animals in the wild will be in the future.

There are good zoos and bad zoos. Good zoos provide living conditions that are clean and as natural as possible. They provide quality food and medical care. Bad zoos exist simply for human entertainment. Living conditions are small and often dirty. Animals are on display rather than living in habitats where they can roam and interact with others of their kind.

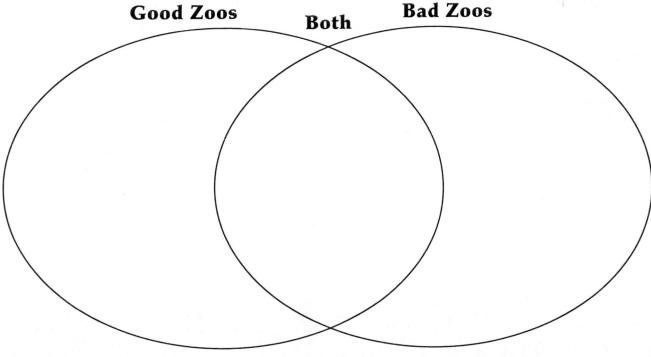

Good Zoos   **Both**   **Bad Zoos**

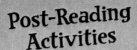
Culminating Activity: Remembering Ivan (cont.)

Directions: Zoo Atlanta has a web page dedicated to Ivan. The site includes photos and videos of the real Ivan. Explore the web page and answer the questions.

> ### Zoo Atlanta Website—Celebrating Ivan
> ### http://www.zooatlanta.org/ivan

1. What kind of gorilla was Ivan?

   _____

   _____

2. How long did Ivan live at Zoo Atlanta?

   _____

   _____

3. Watch the video of Ivan. What does he do in the video?

   _____

   _____

4. How do people still show their love and care for Ivan even though he is gone?

   _____

   _____

Culminating Activity: Remembering Ivan (cont.)

Directions: Learning about Ivan's life teaches you about some bad things humans can do to animals for the sake of entertainment. The last part of Ivan's life showed good things humans can do and how they can care for and help to preserve the lives of wild animals. Create a poster to help others remember Ivan.

Name _____ Date _____

Comprehension Assessment

Directions: Fill in the bubble for the best response to each question.

Section 1—Ivan at the Big Top Mall

1. Who are Ivan's two best friends at the Big Top Mall?

   (A) Ruby and Stella

   (B) Stella and Bob

   (C) Mack and George

   (D) Bob and Julia

Section 2—Ruby and Stella

2. What do Ruby and Stella do that shows they like each other?

   (E) "Ruby picks up a piece of hay."

   (F) "Stella looks so happy."

   (G) Ruby and Stella "sway as if they're dancing."

   (H) Stella "pokes her trunk into the emptiness."

Section 3—Keeping the Promise

3. What is Ivan's promise to Stella?

   (A) He will get himself to a zoo.

   (B) He will help Bob find a home.

   (C) He will make sure Ruby has enough to eat.

   (D) He will make sure Ruby does not live her life in a cage.

Comprehension Assessment *(cont.)*

Section 4—The Plan Works!

4. Describe what the people from the zoo do to help Ivan and Ruby go into the boxes.

_____

_____

_____

_____

_____

_____

Section 5—A New Life for All

5. How does Ivan know that Ruby is happy in her new home?

   (A) He sees Ruby on TV playing with other elephants.

   (B) The zookeepers take him to the elephant habitat.

   (C) Bob tells him she is happy.

   (D) He does not ever know if she is happy.

Name _____ Date _____

Response to Literature:
Favorite Part of the Story

Directions: What is your favorite part of *The One and Only Ivan*? Draw a picture of your favorite scene and write three sentences describing it. Then, answer the questions about your picture on the next page.

```



```

_____

_____

_____

_____

Name _____ Date _____

Response to Literature:
Favorite Part of the Story (cont.)

1. Why is this your favorite part of the story?

_____

_____

_____

_____

2. Does this scene happen at the beginning, middle, or end of the story?

_____

_____

3. What message does this part of the story communicate?

_____

_____

_____

_____

Name _____ Date _____

Response to Literature Rubric

Directions: Use this rubric to evaluate student responses.

Great Job	Good Work	Keep Trying
☐ You answered all three questions completely. You included many details.	☐ You answered all three questions.	☐ You did not answer all three questions.
☐ Your handwriting is very neat. There are no spelling errors.	☐ Your handwriting can be neater. There are some spelling errors.	☐ Your handwriting is not very neat. There are many spelling errors.
☐ Your picture is neat and fully colored.	☐ Your picture is neat and some of it is colored.	☐ Your picture is not very neat and/or fully colored.
☐ Creativity is clear in both the picture and the writing.	☐ Creativity is clear in either the picture or the writing.	☐ There is not much creativity in either the picture or the writing.

Teacher Comments: _____

_____

_____

_____

Name _____ **Date** _____

_____

```
┌─────────────────────────────────────────────┐
│                                               │
│                                               │
│                                               │
│                                               │
│                                               │
│                                               │
│                                               │
│                                               │
│                                               │
└─────────────────────────────────────────────┘
```

_____

_____

_____

_____

_____

_____

_____

_____

Name _____ Date _____

_____

_____

_____

_____

_____

_____

_____

_____

_____

_____

_____

_____

_____

_____

_____

#40101—Instructional Guide: The One and Only Ivan

The responses provided here are just examples of what students may answer. Many accurate responses are possible for the questions throughout this unit.

Vocabulary Activity—Section 1:
Ivan at the Big Top Mall (page 15)
- The Big Top Mall is nothing like a **jungle**.
- Ivan is a mighty **silverback**.
- He was captured when he was a **juvenile**.
- He lives in a **domain** at the Big Top Mall.
- Julia uses her **imagination** to draw pictures.
1. Ivan likes Stella, Bob, and drawing pictures.

Guided Close Reading—Section 1:
Ivan at the Big Top Mall (page 18)
1. He is happy to get paper and crayons from Julia. He draws pictures of the things he sees.
2. Ivan draws the things he sees, but Julia draws things she sees in her mind using her imagination.
3. He says that he saw shapes in the clouds and drew pictures with mud when he was young and living with his family. He thinks that being an artist is part of who he is.

Language Learning—Section 1:
Ivan at the Big Top Mall (page 20)
1. Stella is a mountain.
2. Bob is a mouse.
3. The seal is a clown.
4. The sun bear is a cottonball.
5. The gorilla is an otter.

Story Elements—Section 1:
Ivan at the Big Top Mall (page 21)

	Ivan	Stella	Bob
Where does he or she come from?	Ivan comes from Africa.	Stella lived in a place with leafy canopies, mist, and waterfalls.	Bob was dumped on the freeway as a puppy.
How does he or she end up at the Big Top Mall?	Mack brought Ivan to the Big Top Mall when he got too big to live at his house.	She came to the Big Top Mall after being in the circus.	He found his way into the Big Top Mall and into Ivan's cage through a hole in the wall.
What is something special about him or her?	Ivan cares about his friends, and he is an artist.	Stella remembers everything. She is a good friend to Ivan.	Bob is a good friend to Ivan.

List one or two things he or she likes at the Big Top Mall.	He likes Bob and Stella. He likes drawing.	Stella likes Ivan.	He likes sleeping on Ivan's belly, and he likes being in a place that is warm.
Write three words to describe him or her.	Ivan is big, kind, artistic, and a good friend.	Stella is huge, kind, has a sore leg, and is a good friend to Ivan.	Bob is small, is a good friend to Ivan, and does not like humans.

Vocabulary Activity—Section 2:
Ruby and Stella (page 24)
1. Stella sways against her, and she wraps her trunk around Ruby's trunk.

Guided Close Reading—Section 2:
Ruby and Stella (page 27)
1. Ivan says he likes stories with "cloudless blue-sky endings."
2. Stella says a good zoo is large, safe, and has room to roam. It also has humans who don't hurt animals.
3. Stella says Jambo stood watch over the boy.

Making Connections—Section 2:
Ruby and Stella (page 28)
- **Living in the Wild:** Have to find food; Space to move around; Natural surroundings; Contact with other wild animals; Free to do as they please
- **Living in Captivity:** Food provided; Stuck in a small area; Human-made surroundings; Not much contact with other animals; Kept behind bars or glass

Language Learning—Section 2:
Ruby and Stella (page 29)
1. Stella and Ruby become friends.
2. Ivan lives at the Big Top Mall.
3. Julia gives Ivan paper and crayons.
4. Ivan was born in Africa.
5. The real Ivan lived at Zoo Atlanta.
6. Ruby loves Stella like a mother.

Vocabulary Activity—Section 3:
Keeping the Promise (page 33)
- Ruby is **dozing** after she hits Mack with her trunk.
- Ivan tries to look **encouragingly** at Julia's painting.
- Bob gives a **scornful** laugh about Mack getting hit.
- Ivan tells Ruby that zoos are humans' way of making **amends**.
- Ruby shows **annoyance** at the ropes on her feet.

Guided Close Reading—Section 3:
Keeping the Promise (page 36)
1. He gives a "scornful laugh" when Ruby hits Mack during the training session.
2. Julia asks George if he thinks Mack will hurt Ruby and wonders if they should call someone to help. George says he does not think Mack will hurt Ruby.
3. "He turns away, and only then do I hear him laughing."

Language Learning—Section 3:
Keeping the Promise (page 38)
1. "I can help Ruby," says Ivan.
2. Stella says, "Humans are unpredictable."
3. "I'm happy Ruby hit Mack," Bob growls.
4. "Dad, come see what Ivan created," exclaims Julia.
5. "We've faced a lot together, Ivan," says Mack.

Vocabulary Activity—Section 4:
The Plan Works! (page 42)
1. The billboard sign is a **monstrosity**.
2. The billboard brings **publicity** to Ruby.
3. Saving Ruby is a matter of **principle**.
4. The **protestors** are angry that Ruby lives in a cage.
5. Ivan will be happy that Ruby is in a safe place, but he will probably miss seeing her.

Guided Close Reading—Section 4:
The Plan Works! (page 45)
1. He jumps around his cage and screams.
2. She sees the logo of the red giraffe.
3. George says Mack will fire him. That shows that he knows that he is doing something that Mack will think is wrong.

Language Learning—Section 4:
The Plan Works! (page 47)
1. Ivan's friend
2. Julia's crayons
3. Stella's cage
4. Mack's Big Top Mall
5. Ruby's trunk
6. George's broom

Story Elements—Section 4:
The Plan Works! (page 48)
- The picture should include walls, grass, Ruby, and the word *HOME*.

Story Elements—Section 4:
The Plan Works! (page 49)
- George puts up the billboard.
- Julia calls the newspaper.
- A reporter comes to visit.
- Protestors hold signs outside the Big Top Mall.
- The woman from the zoo visits Ruby.

Vocabulary Activity—Section 5:
A New Life for All (page 51)
1. Ivan is probably afraid of the other gorillas since it has been many years since he has seen another gorilla.

Guided Close Reading—Section 5:
A New Life for All (page 54)
1. He grumbles, swats, swaggers, and beats his chest.
2. Ivan sees her on TV with other elephants. They roll in the mud with her and nuzzle her. He can tell she is happy.
3. Kinyani taps Ivan on the shoulder and runs away.

Making Connections—Section 5:
A New Life for All (page 55)
1. ant
2. bird
3. cloud
4. dirt
5. flower
6. grass
7. rock
8. sky
9. tree
10. wind

Language Learning—Section 5:
A New Life for All (page 56)
1. This elephant is biggest.
2. That giraffe is tallest.
3. Bob is the smallest dog.
4. This gorilla is oldest.
5. Ruby is youngest.
6. Mack is meanest.
7. Stella's tail is longest.

Culminating Activity (page 62)
1. Ivan was a western lowland gorilla.
2. He lived there for 17 years, since 1994.
3. Ivan eats and walks around his enclosure.
4. He still receives birthday and holiday cards.

Comprehension Assessment—Section 5:
A New Life for All (p. 64–65)
1. B. Stella and Bob
2. G. Ruby and Stella "sway as if they're dancing."
3. D. He will make sure Ruby does not live her life in a cage.
4. They use a clicker and treats. Each time Ivan or Ruby touches the box, the people use the clicker and give them treats.
5. A. He sees Ruby on TV playing with other elephants.